Coloring Book For Kids
Awesome Animals

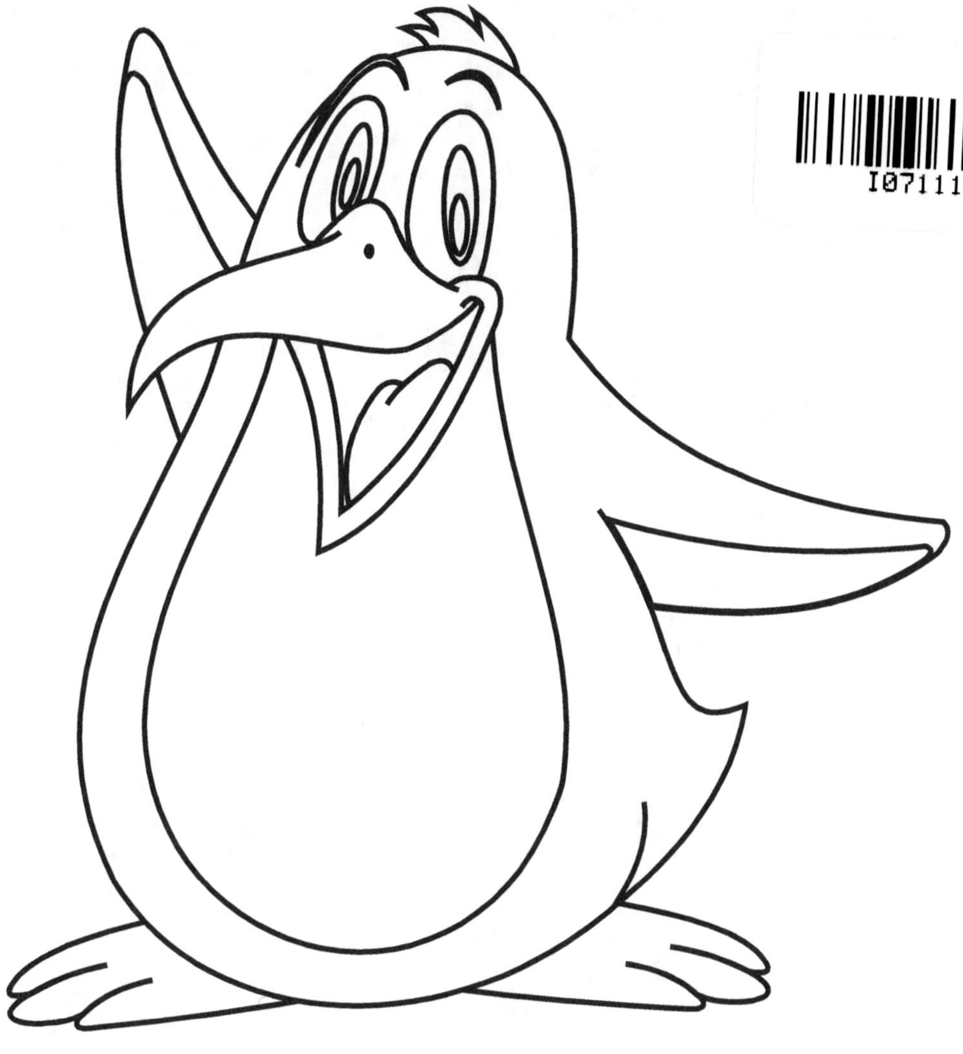

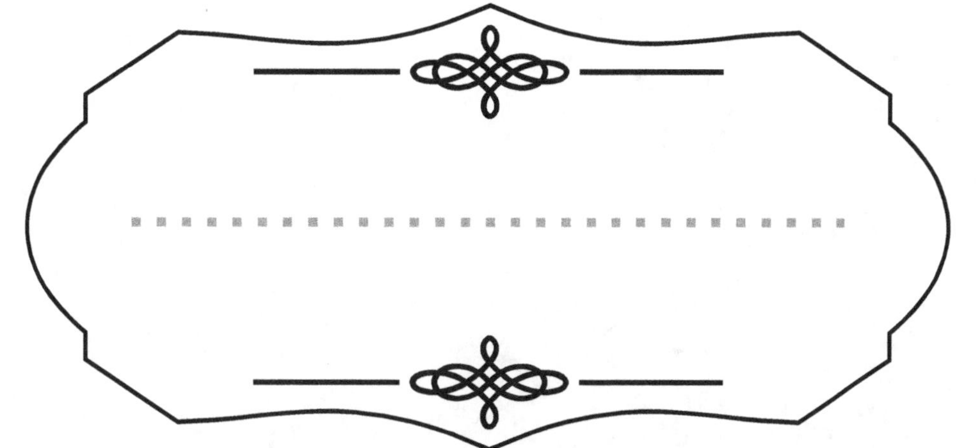

THIS BOOK BELONGS TO :

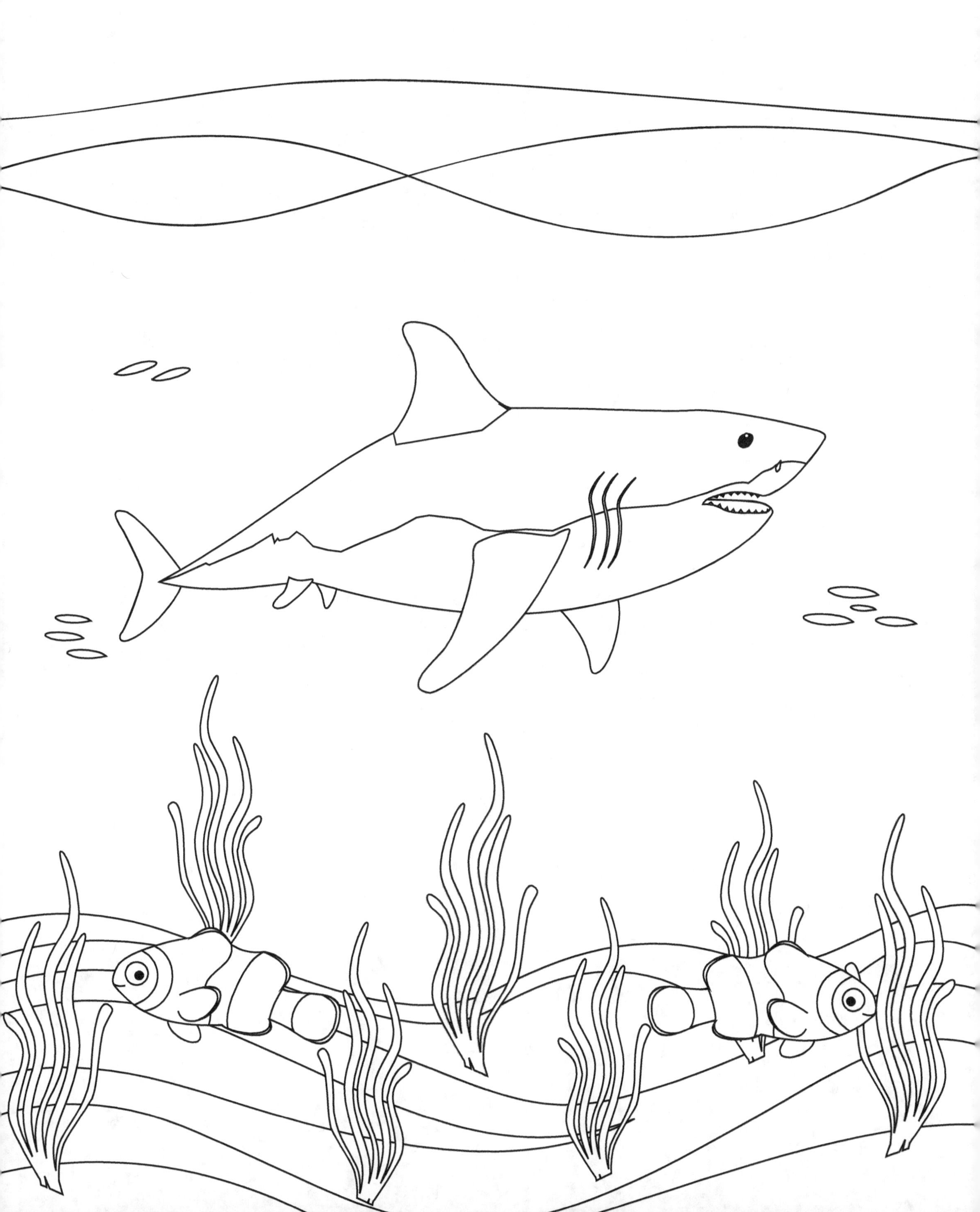

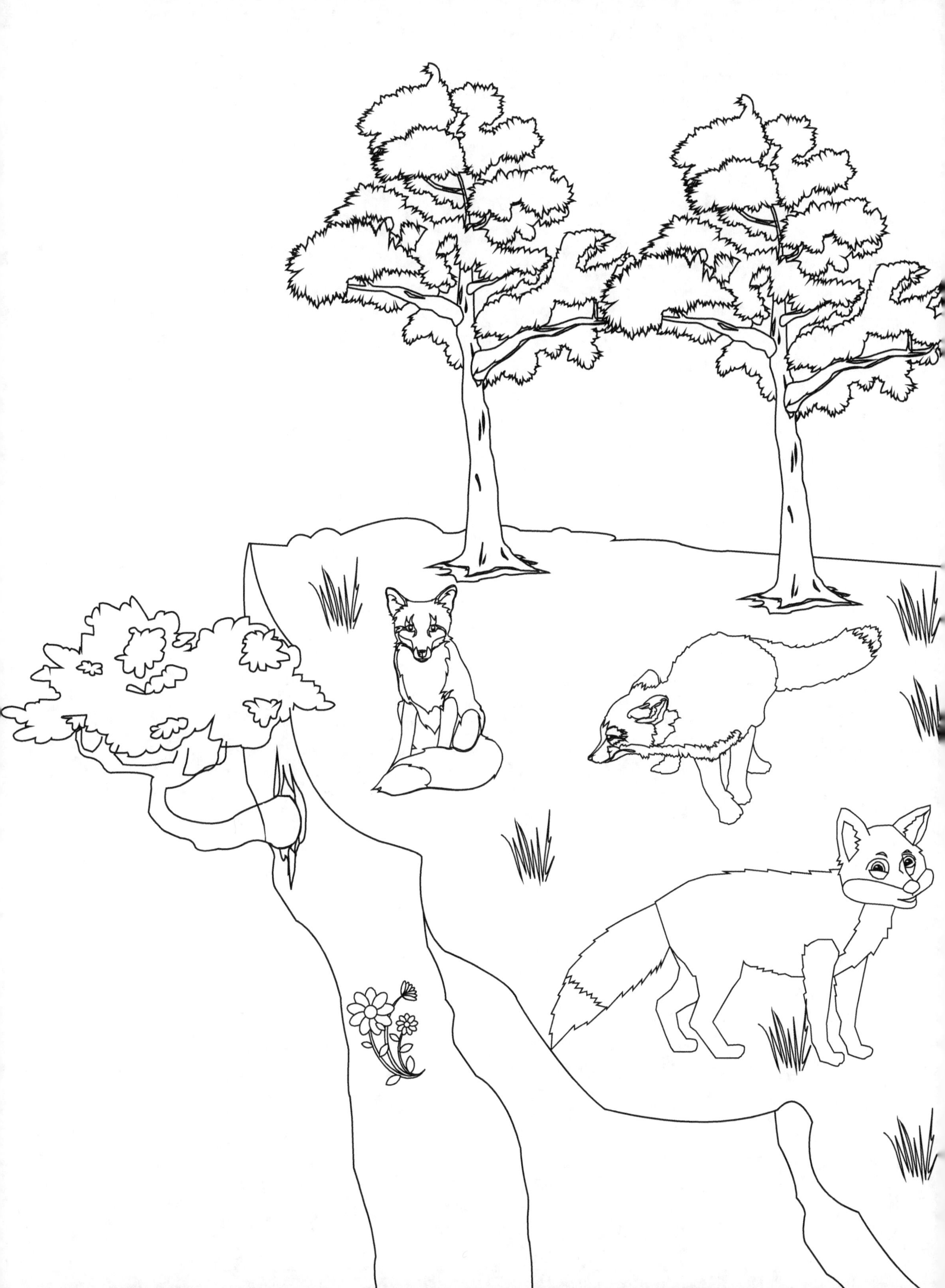

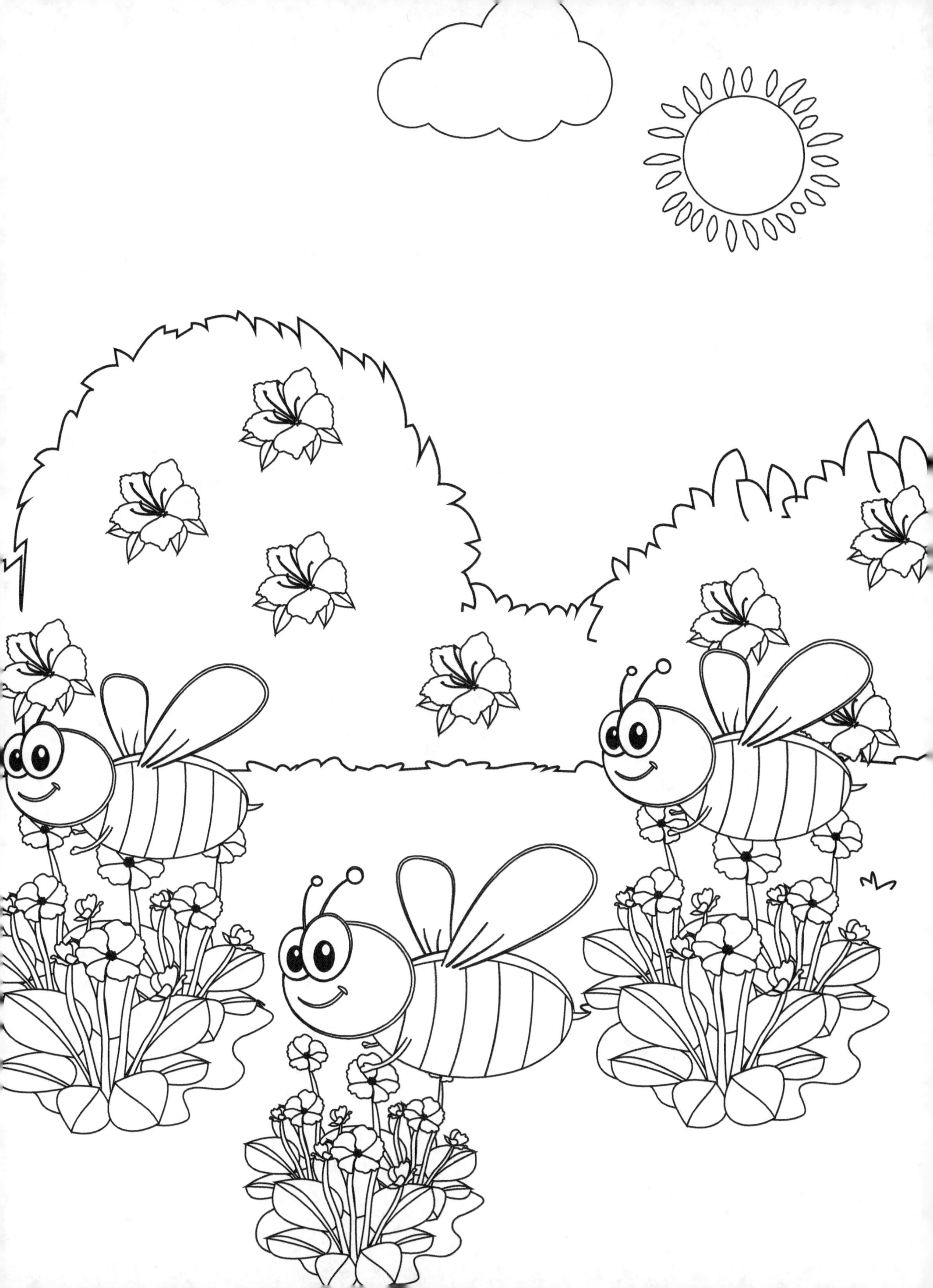

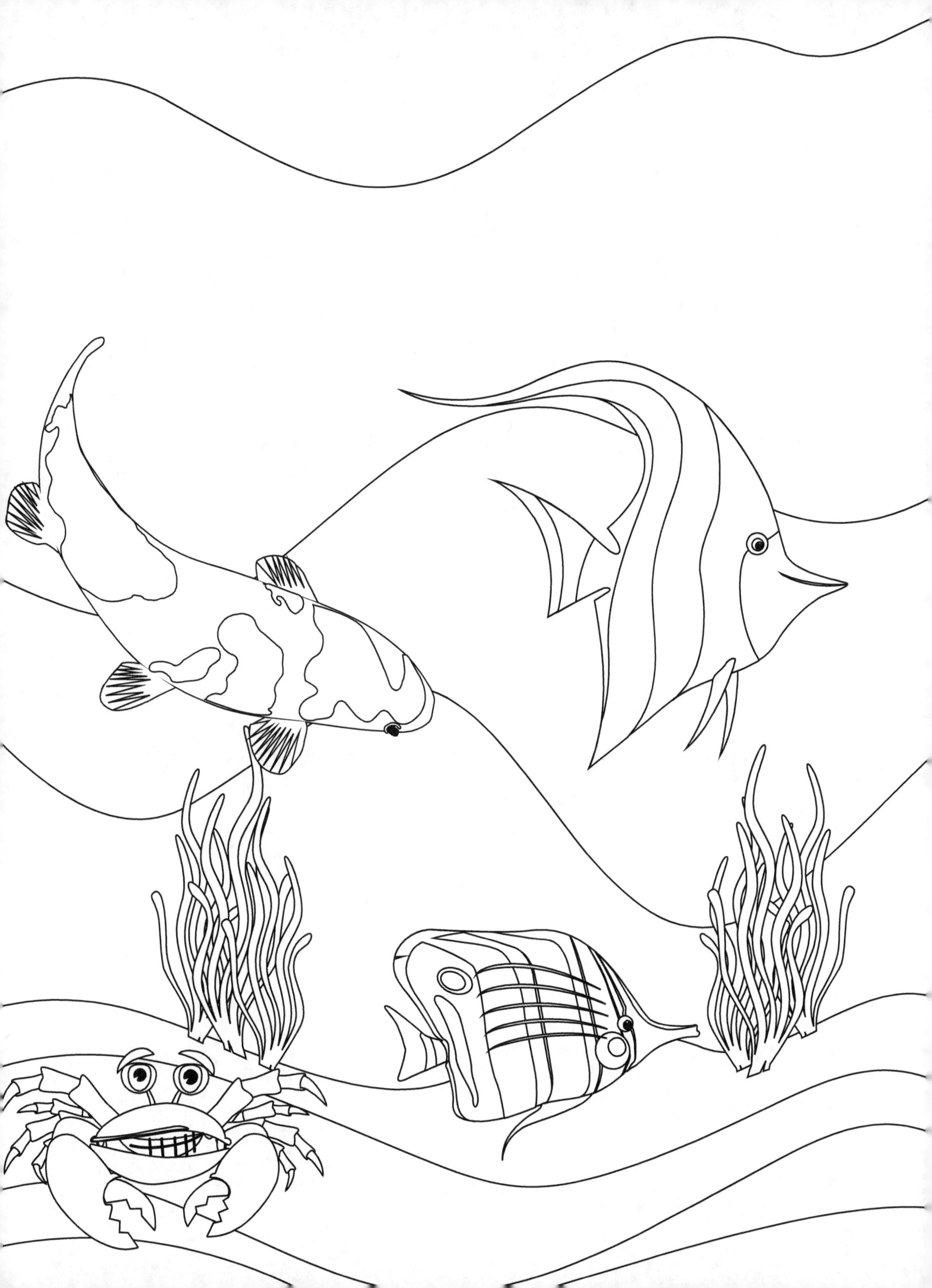

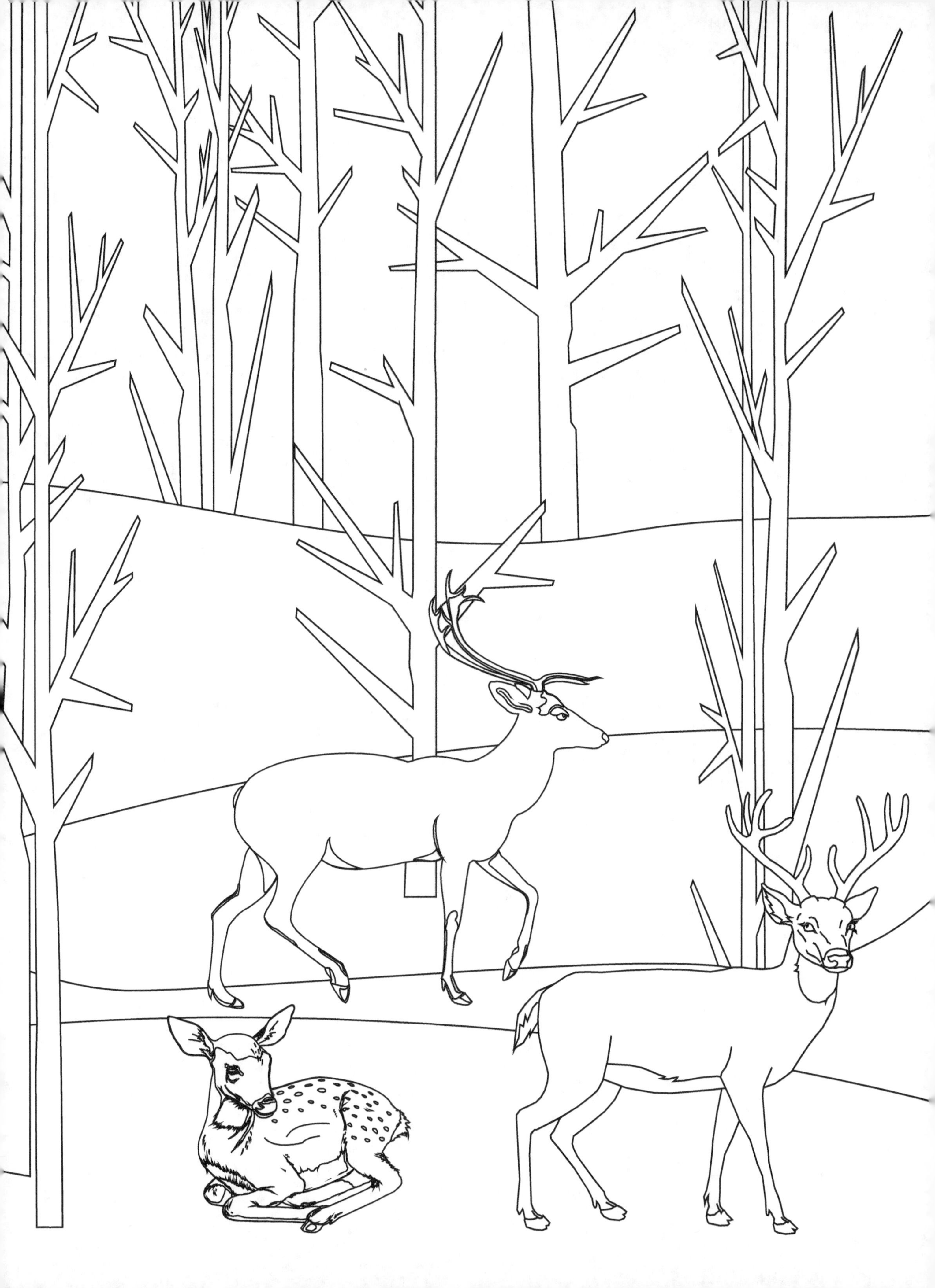

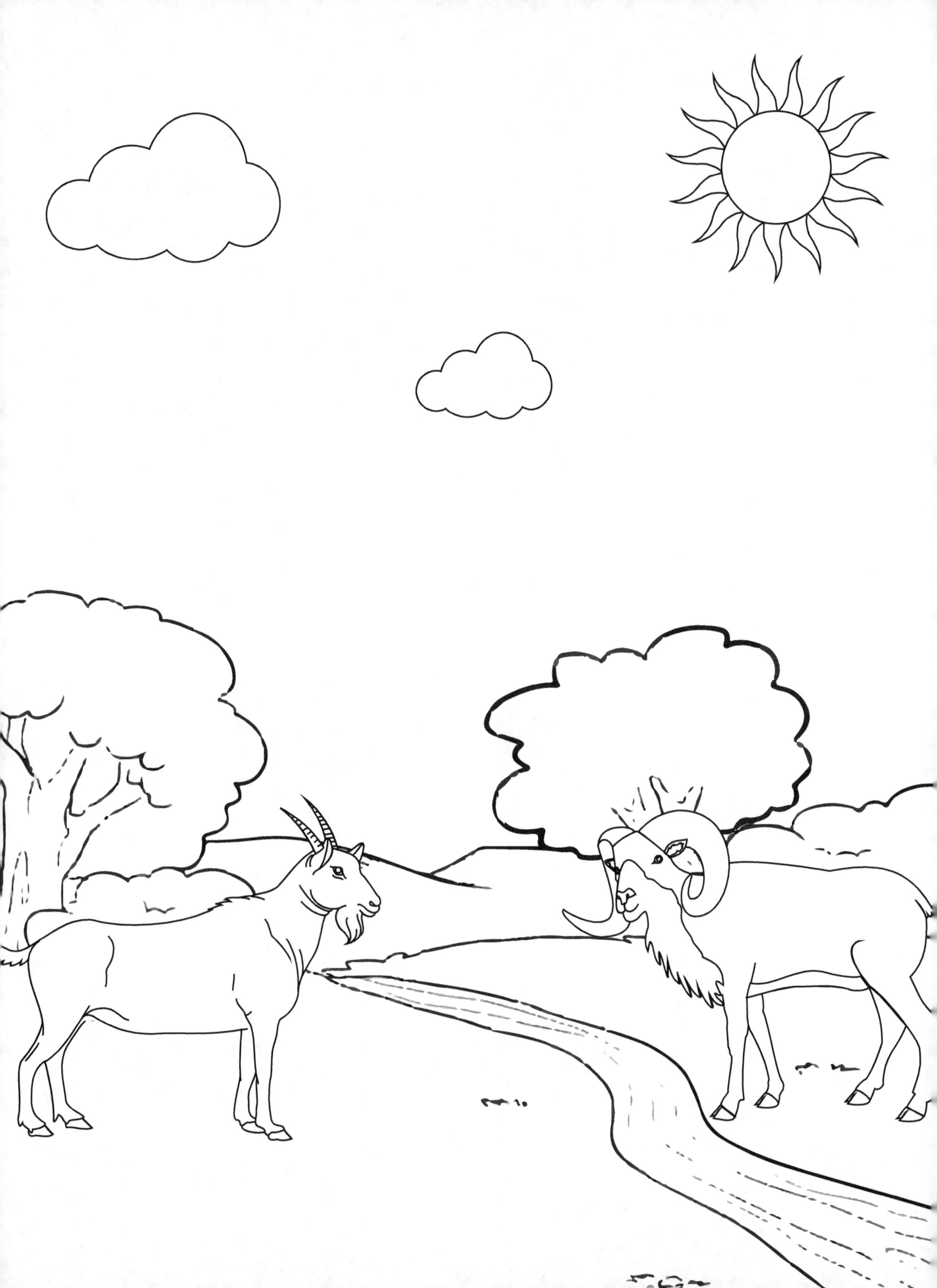

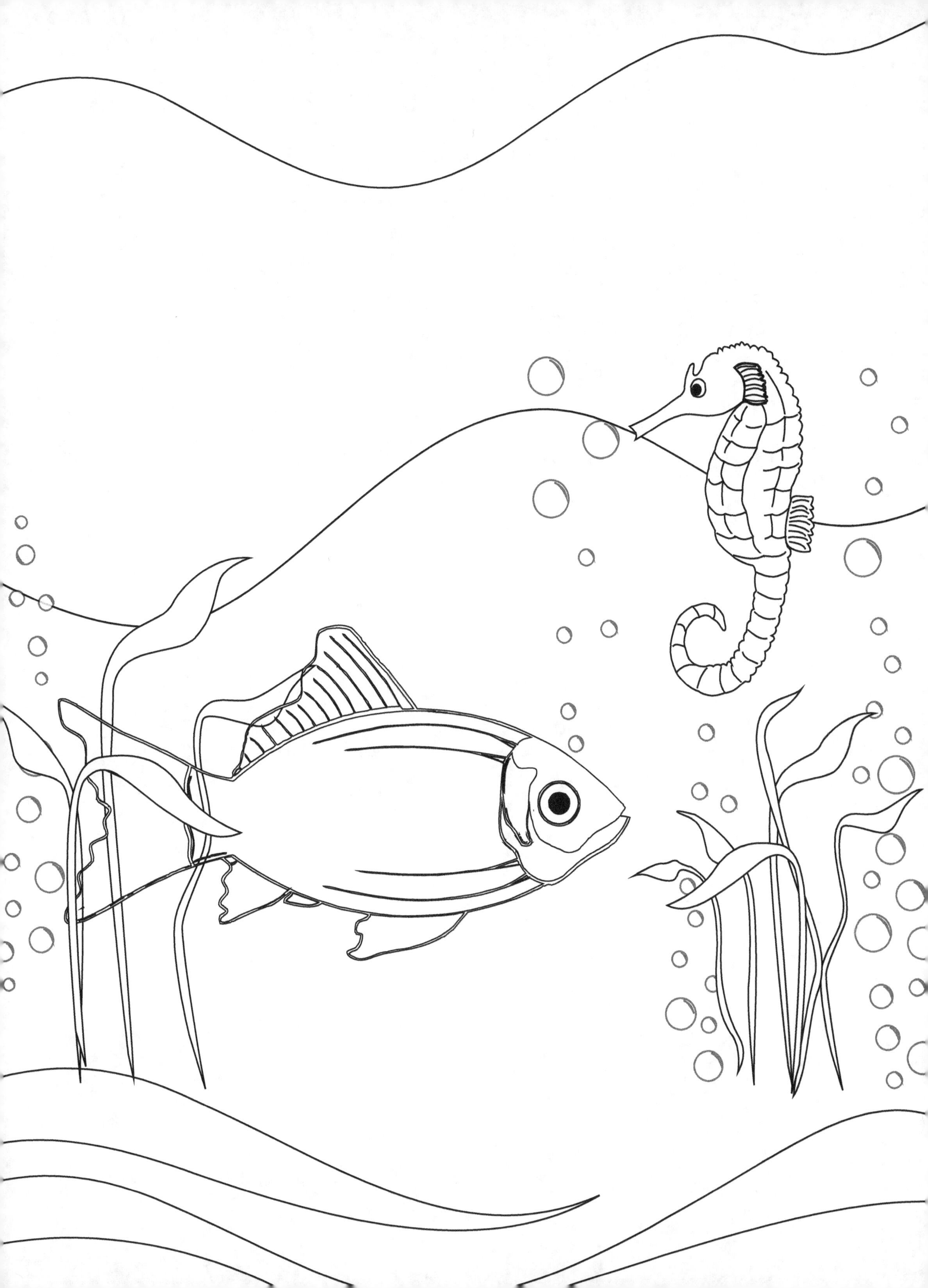

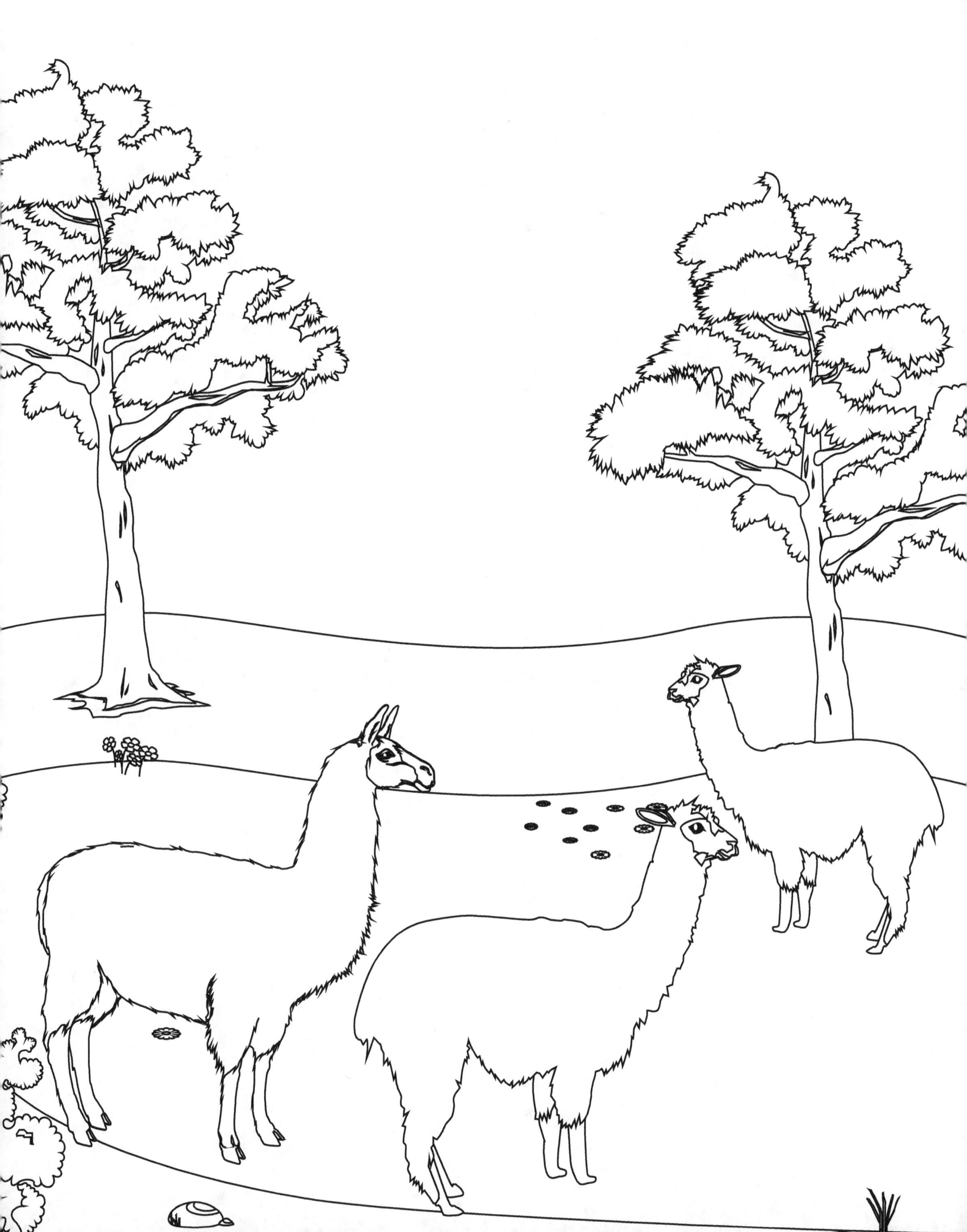

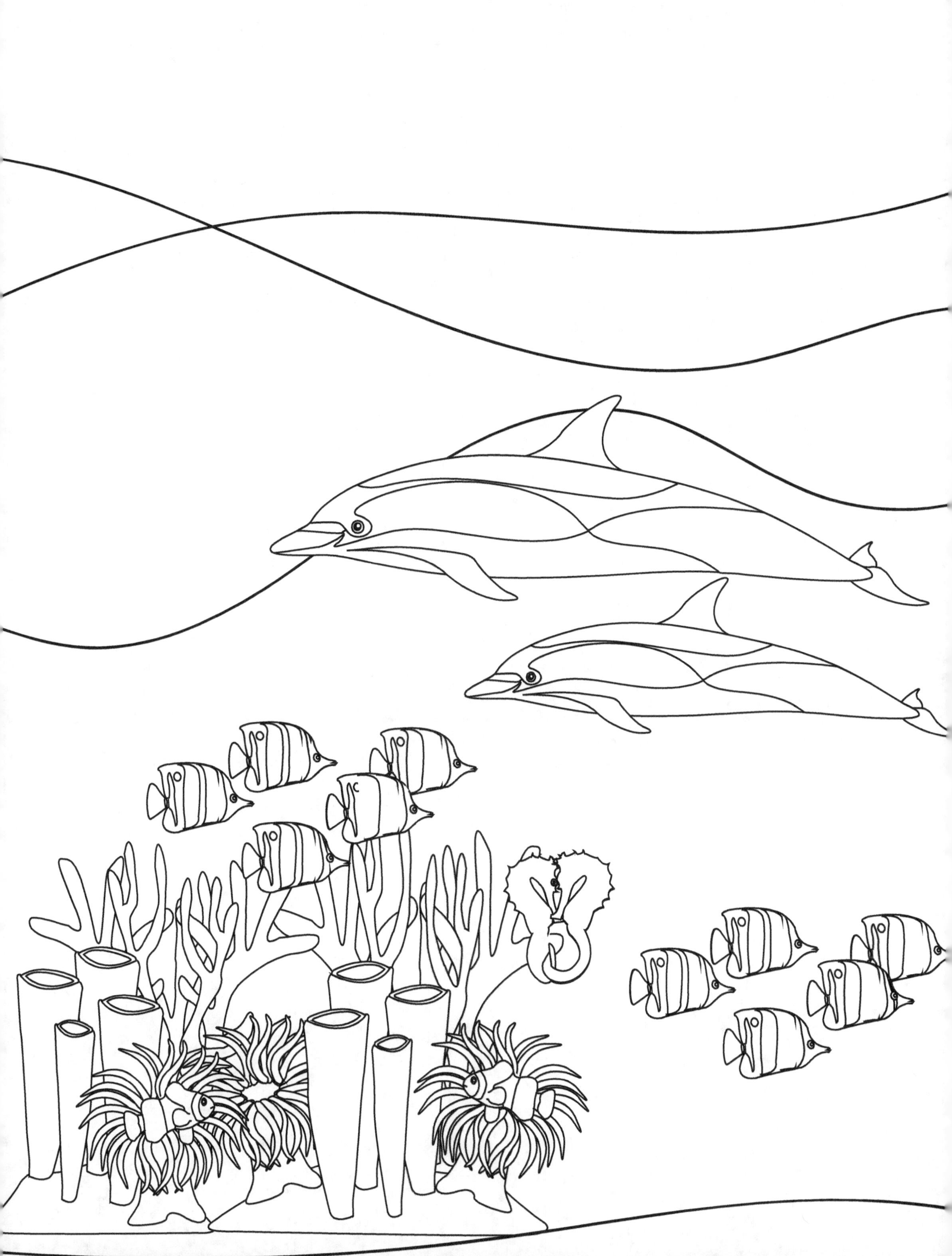

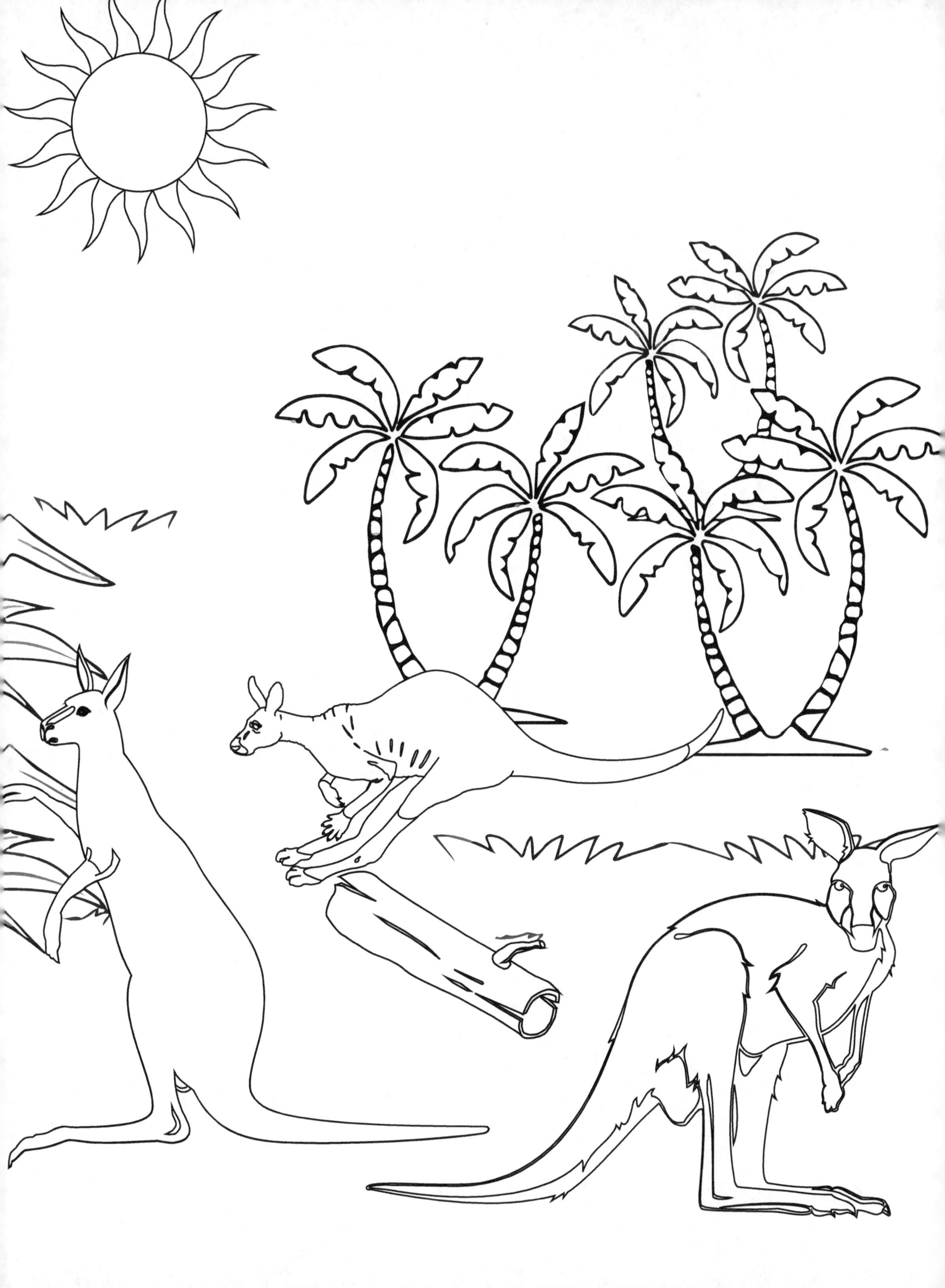

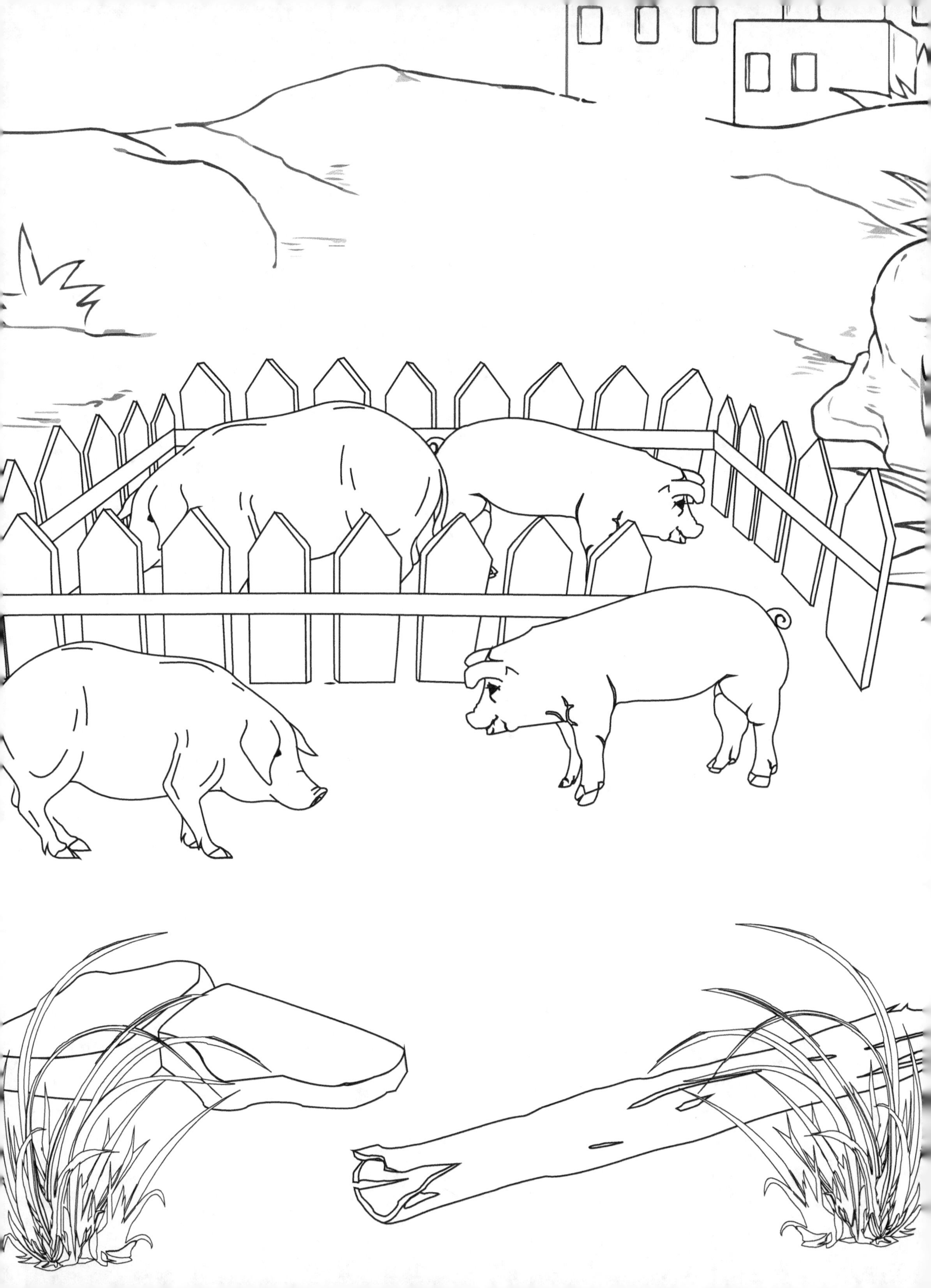

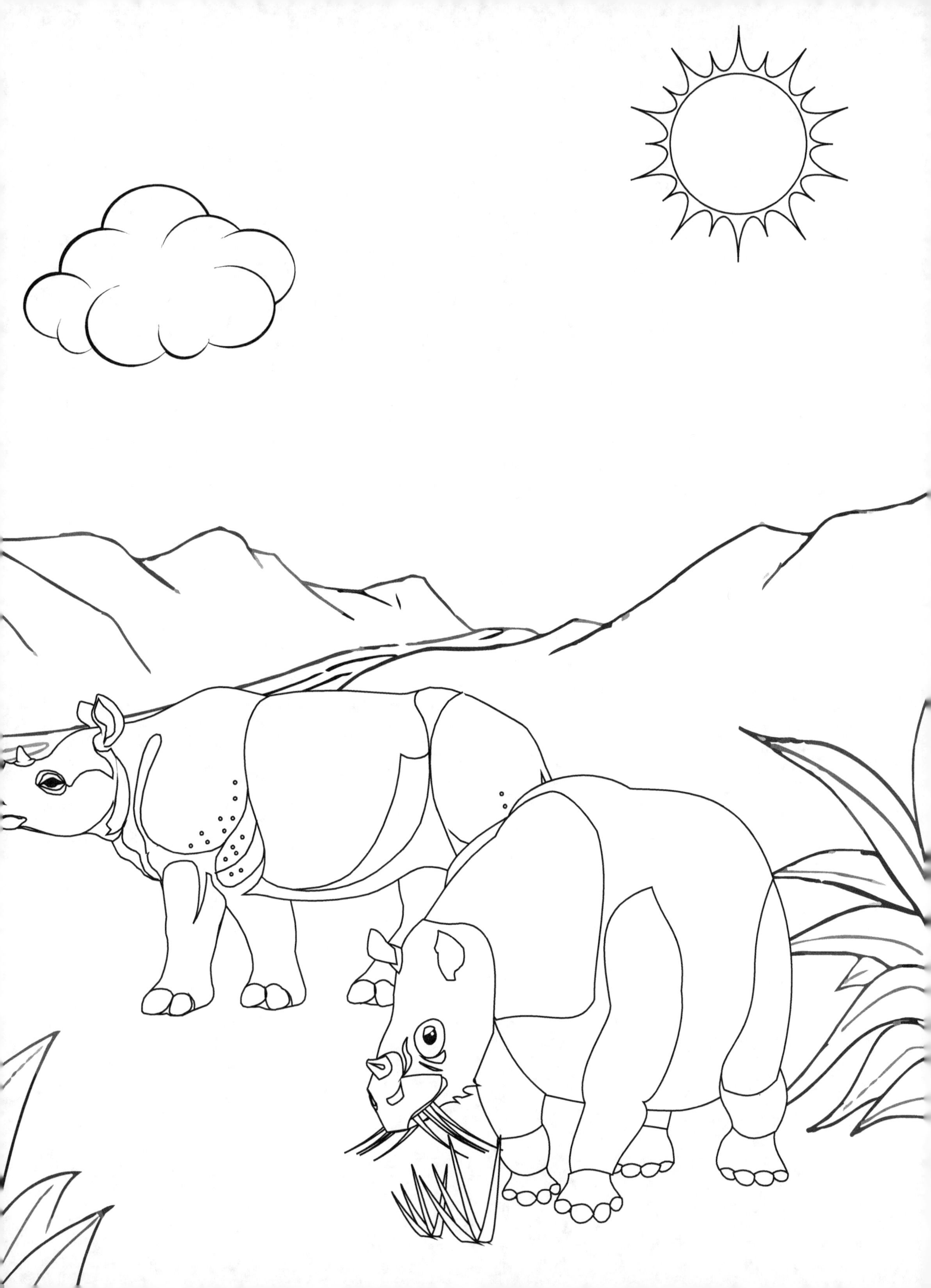

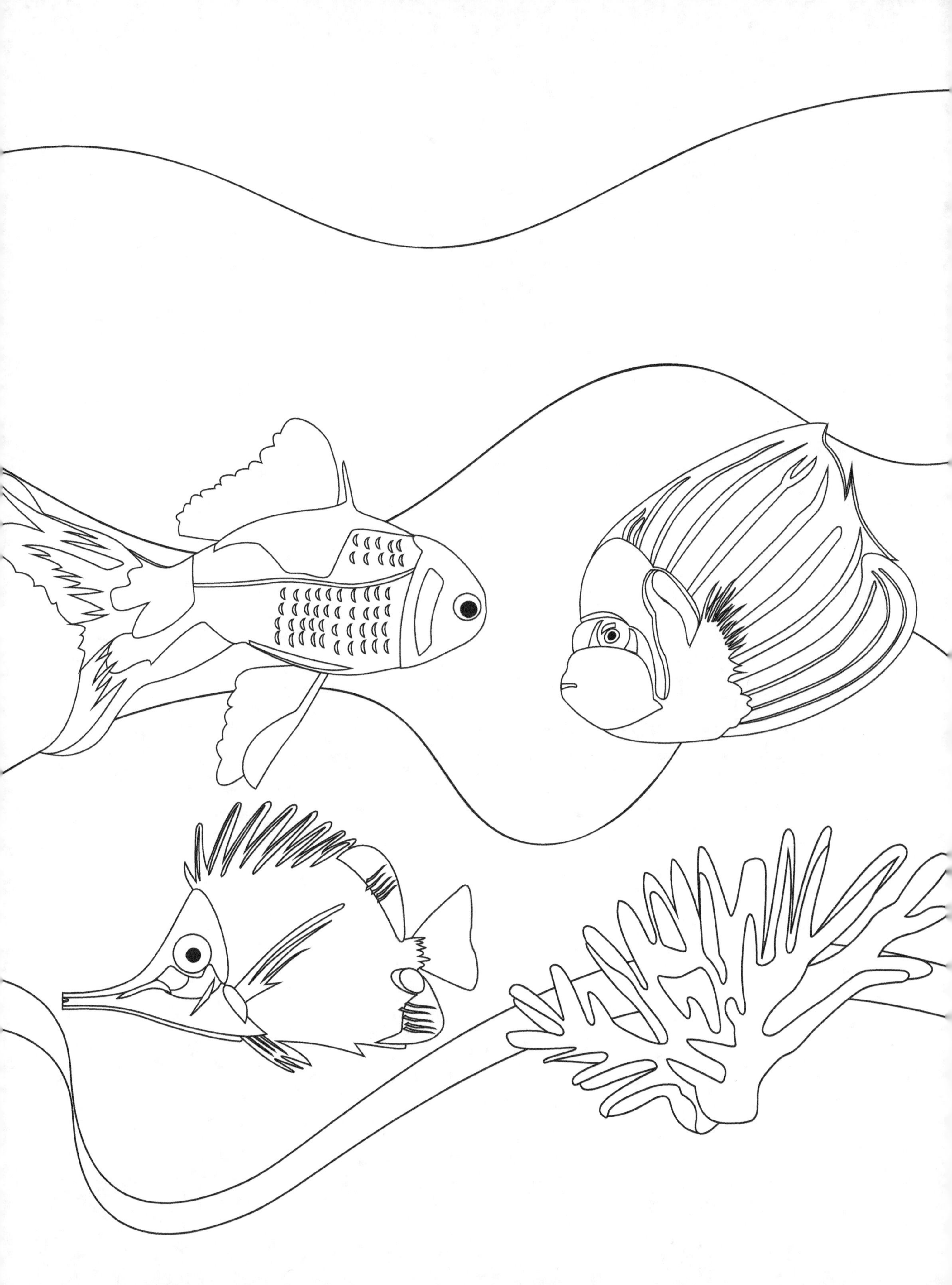

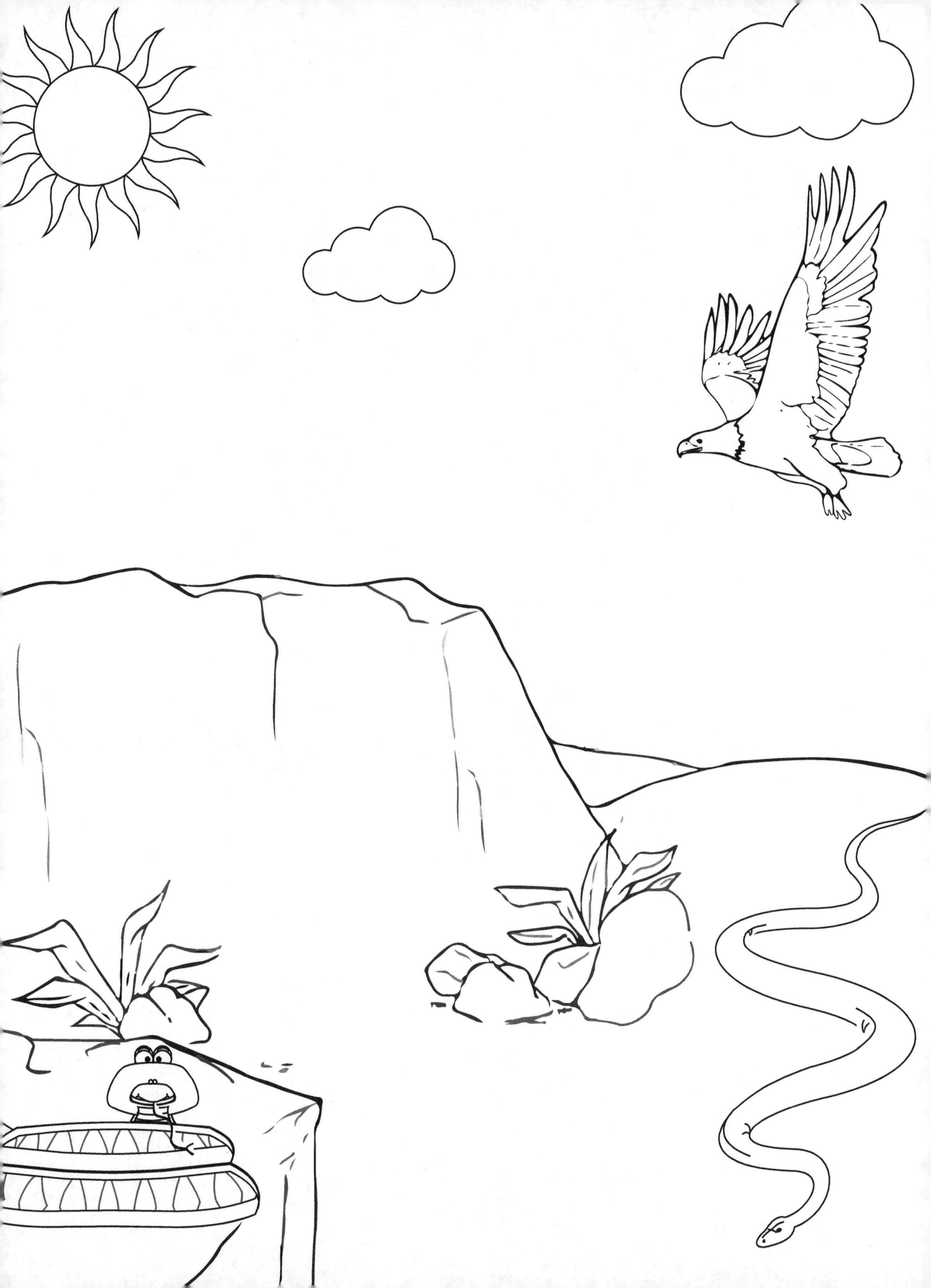

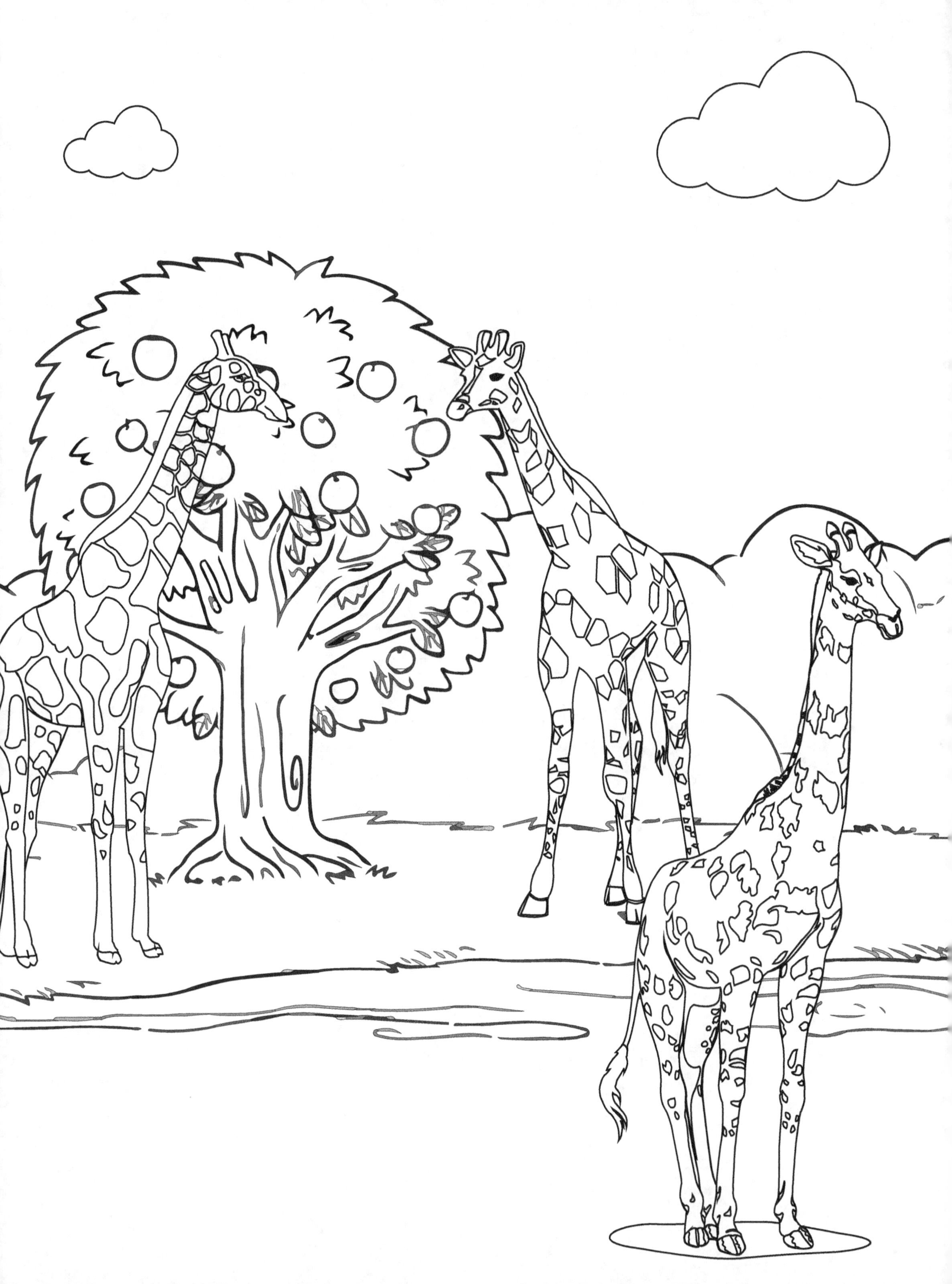

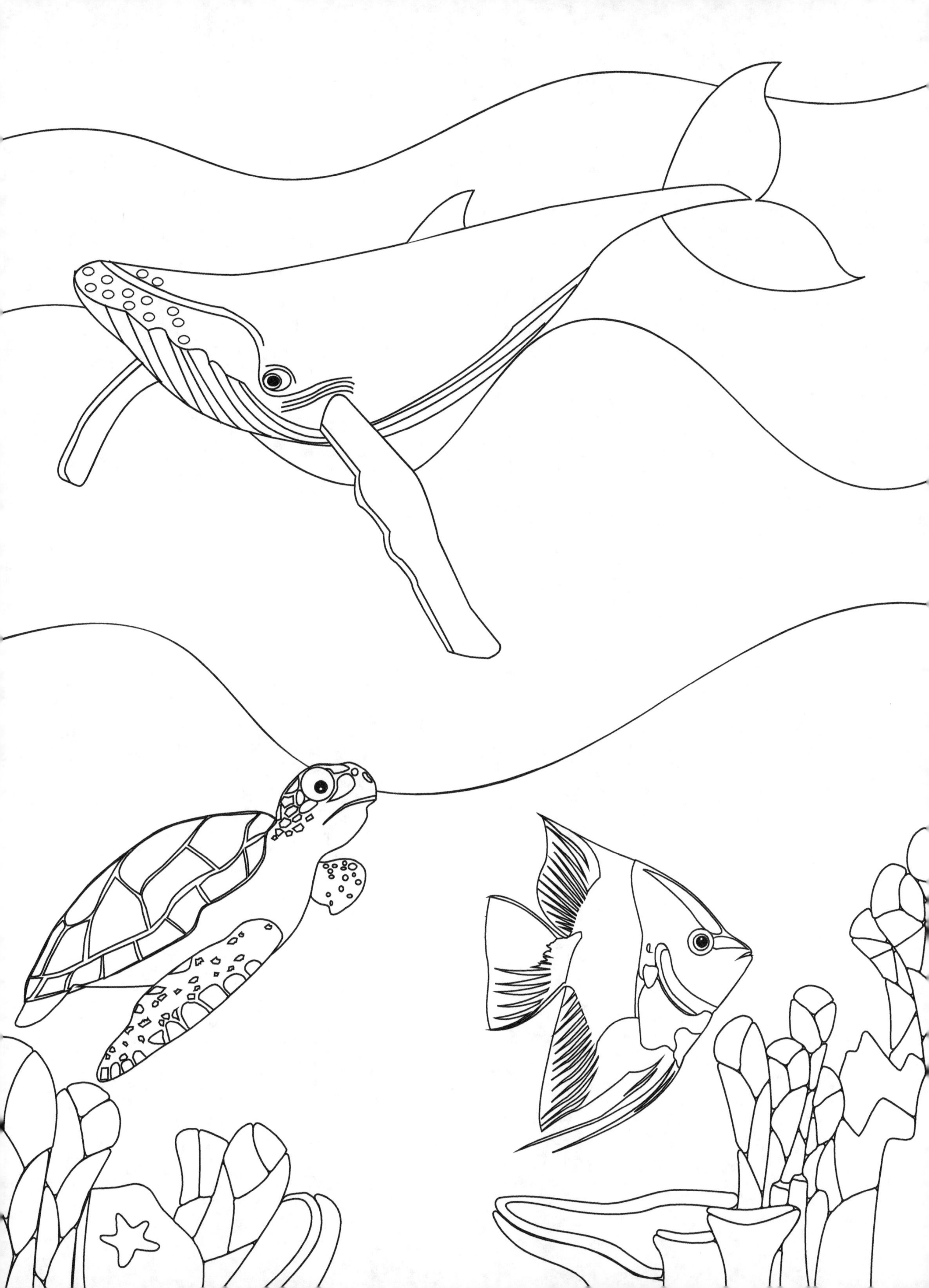

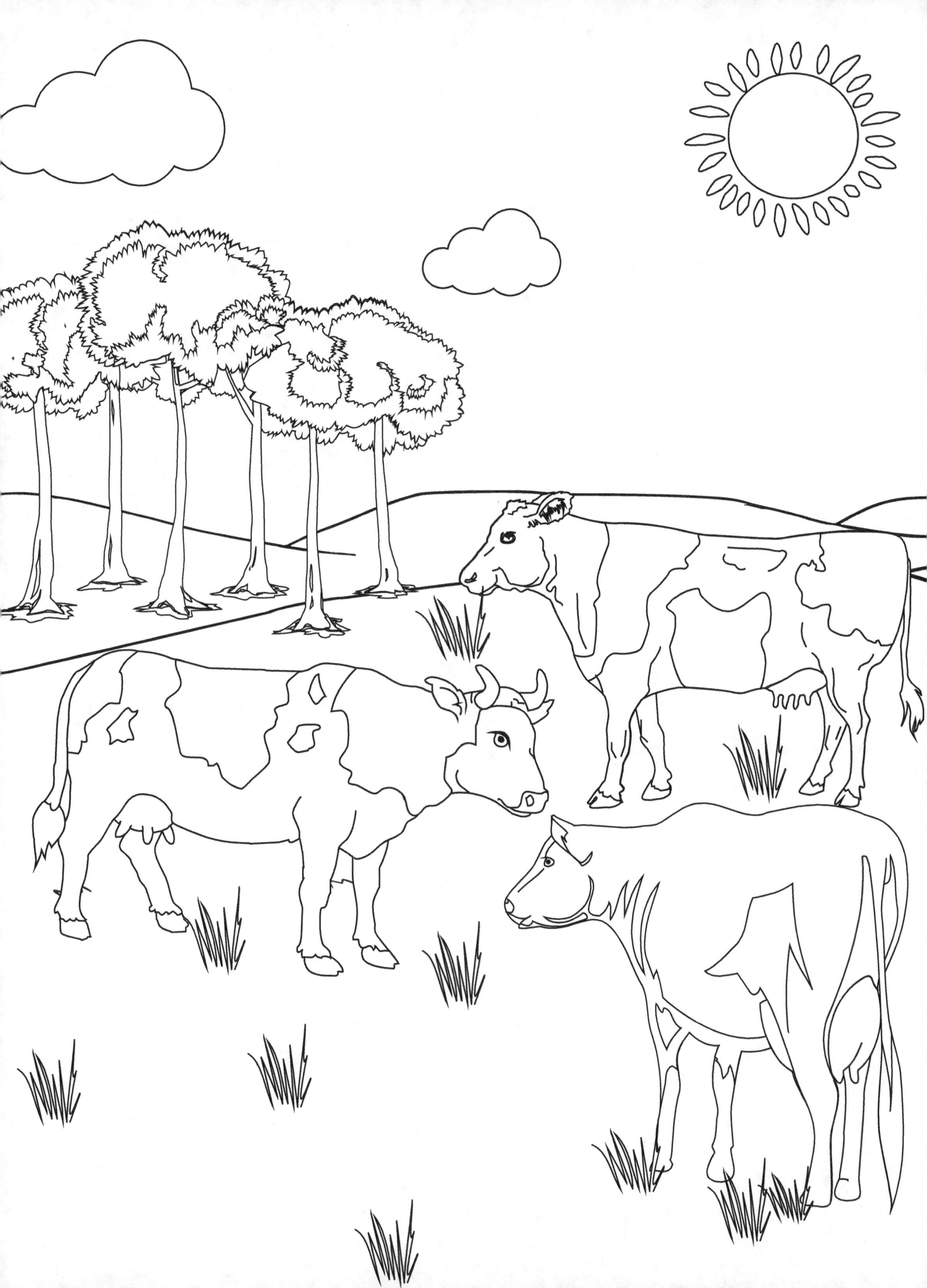

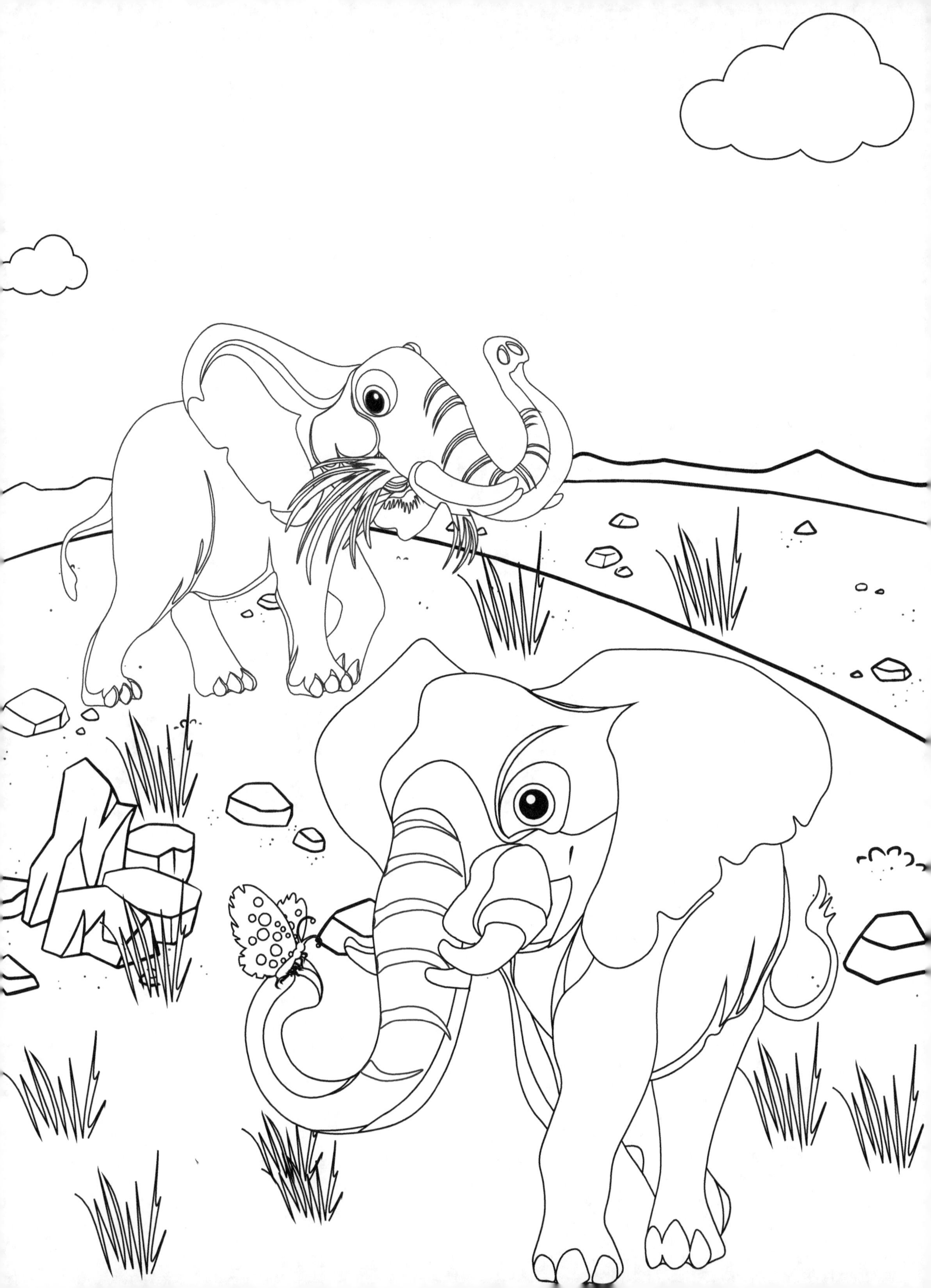

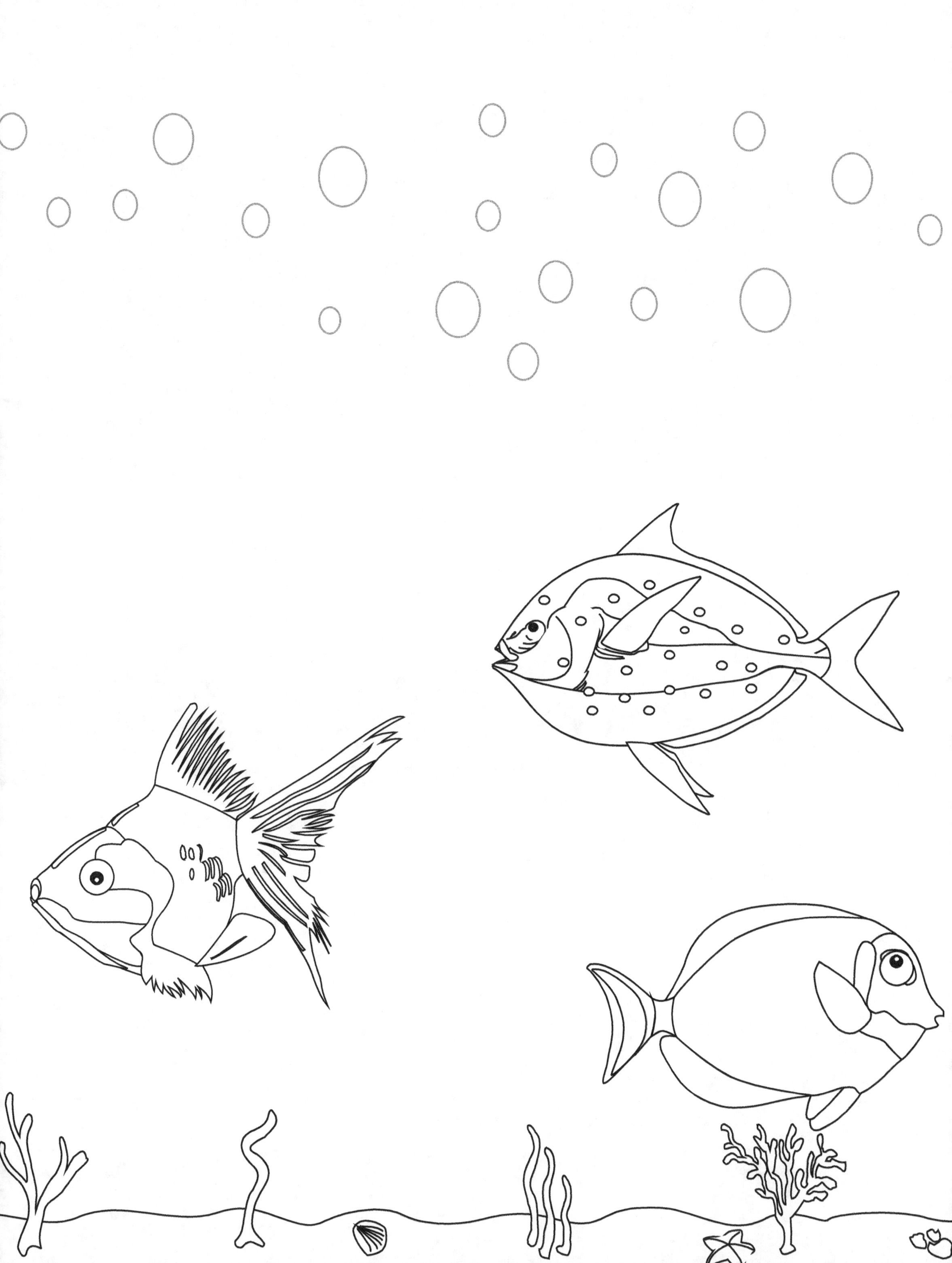

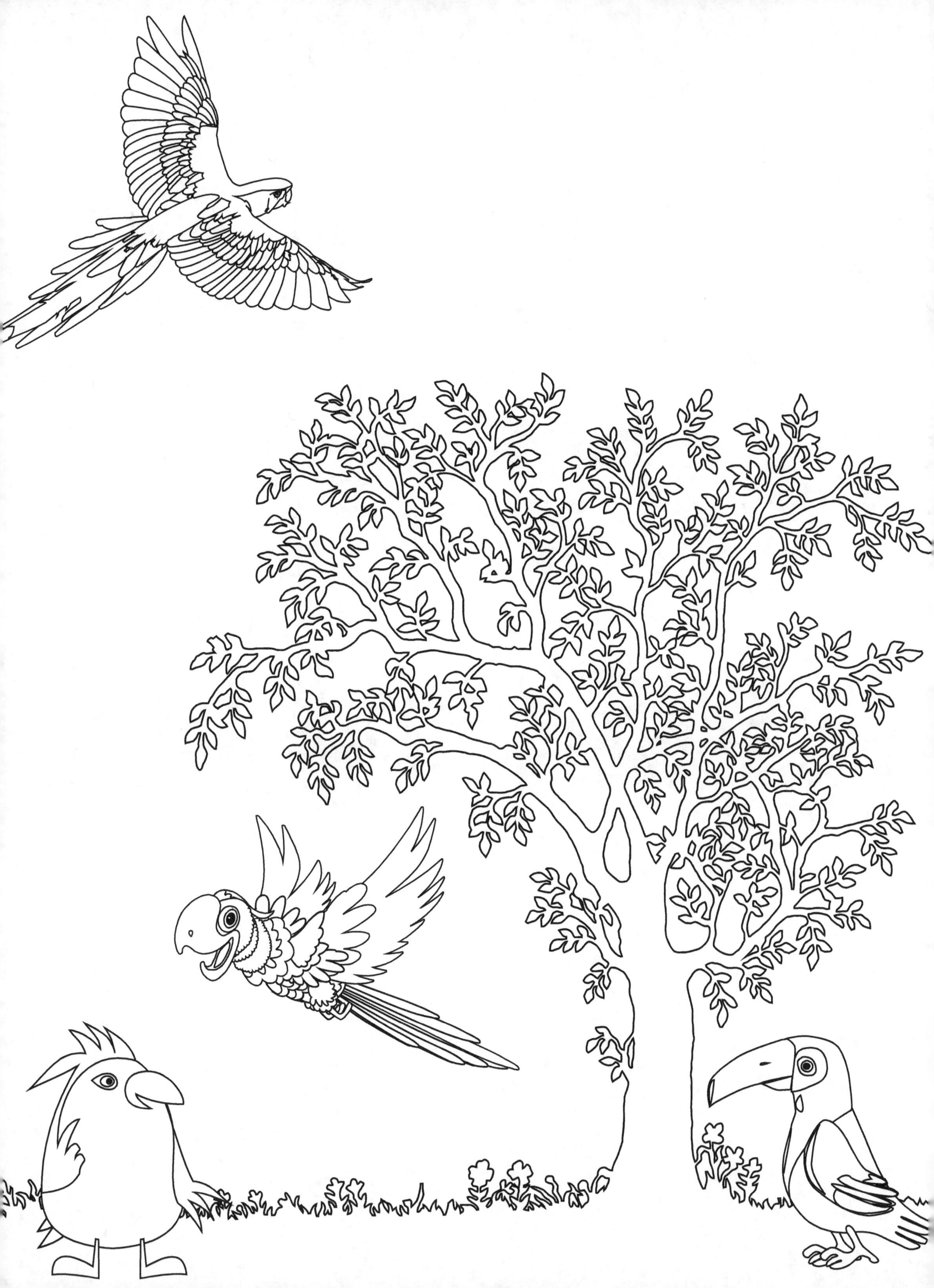

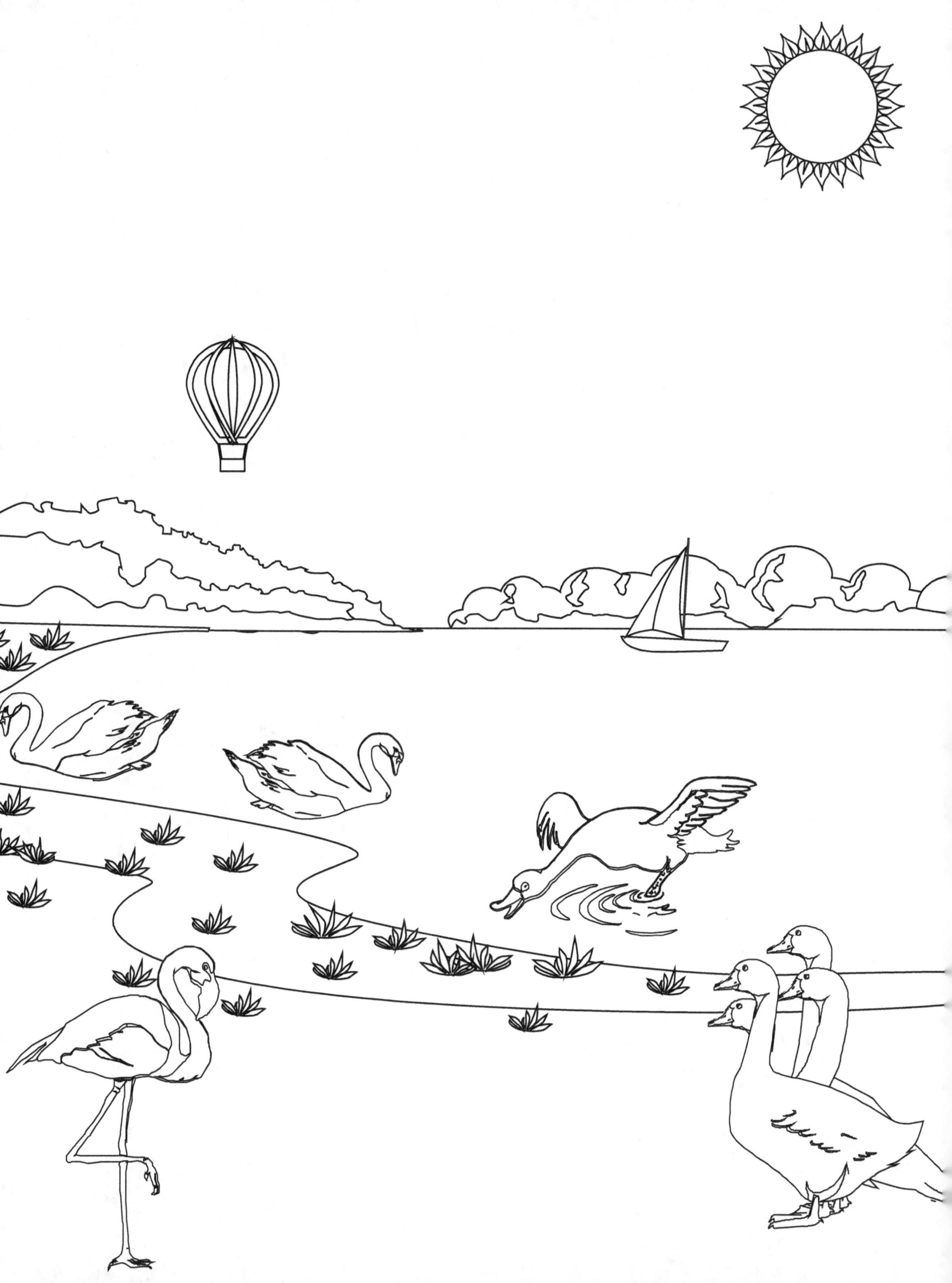

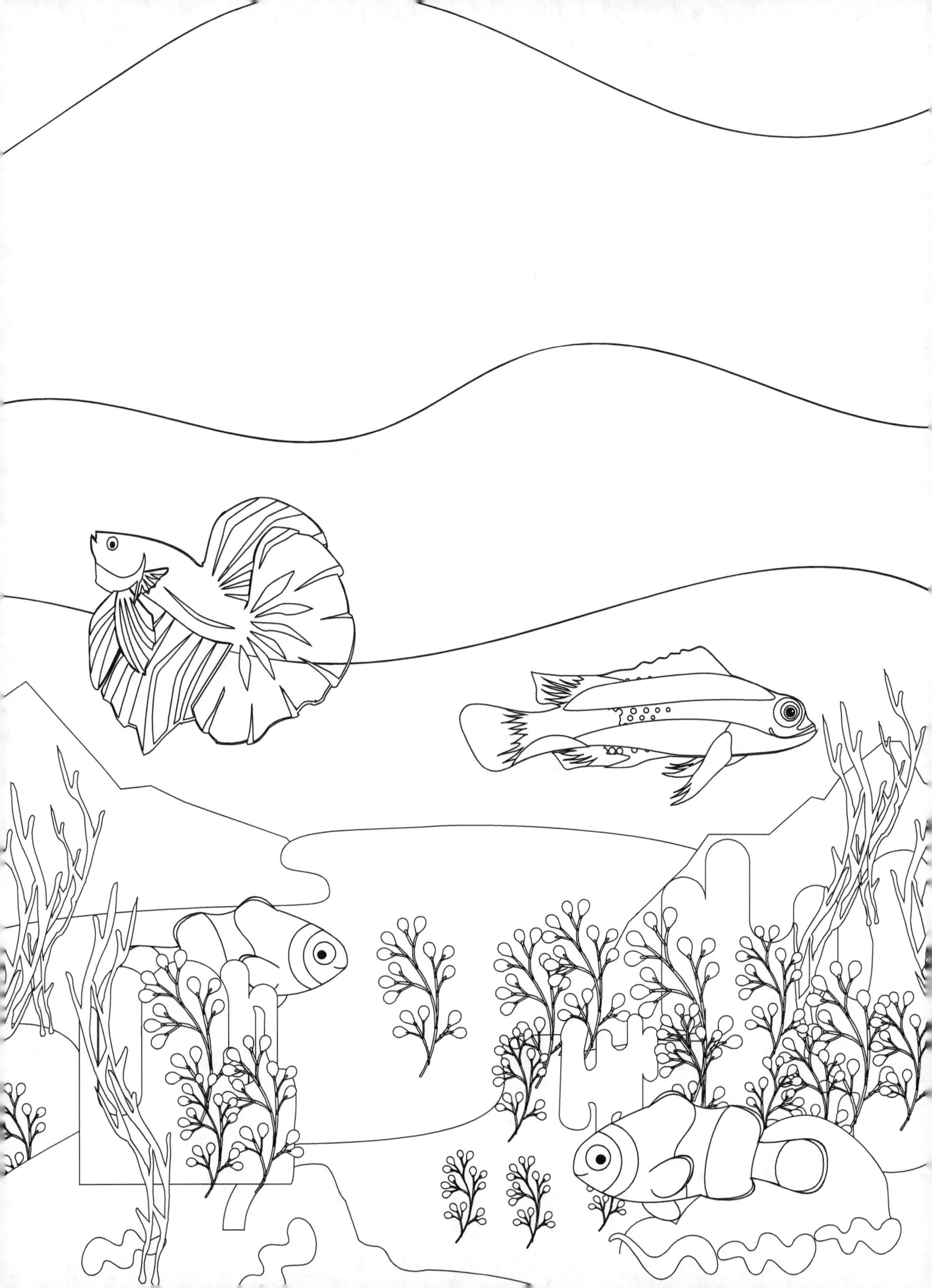

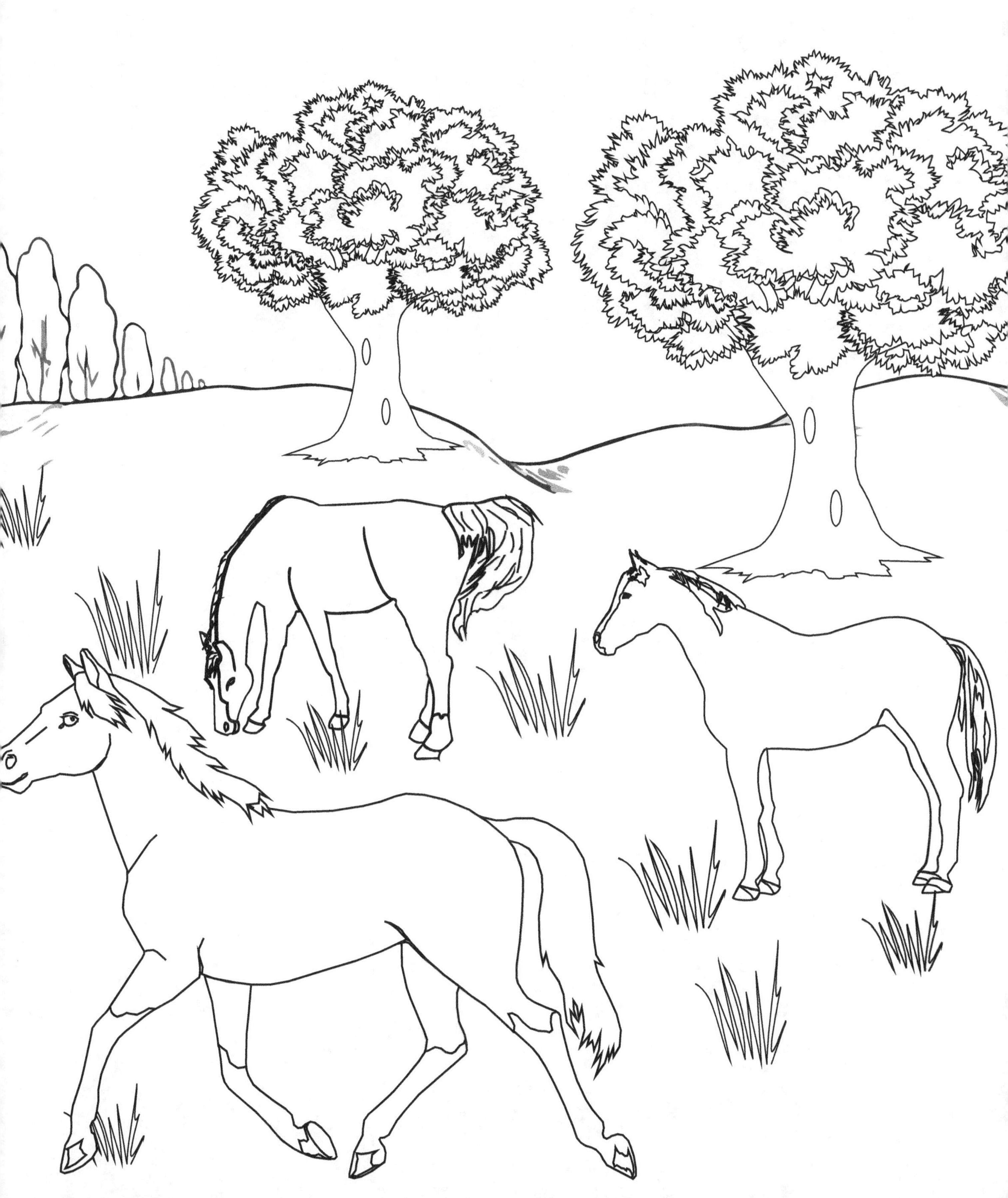

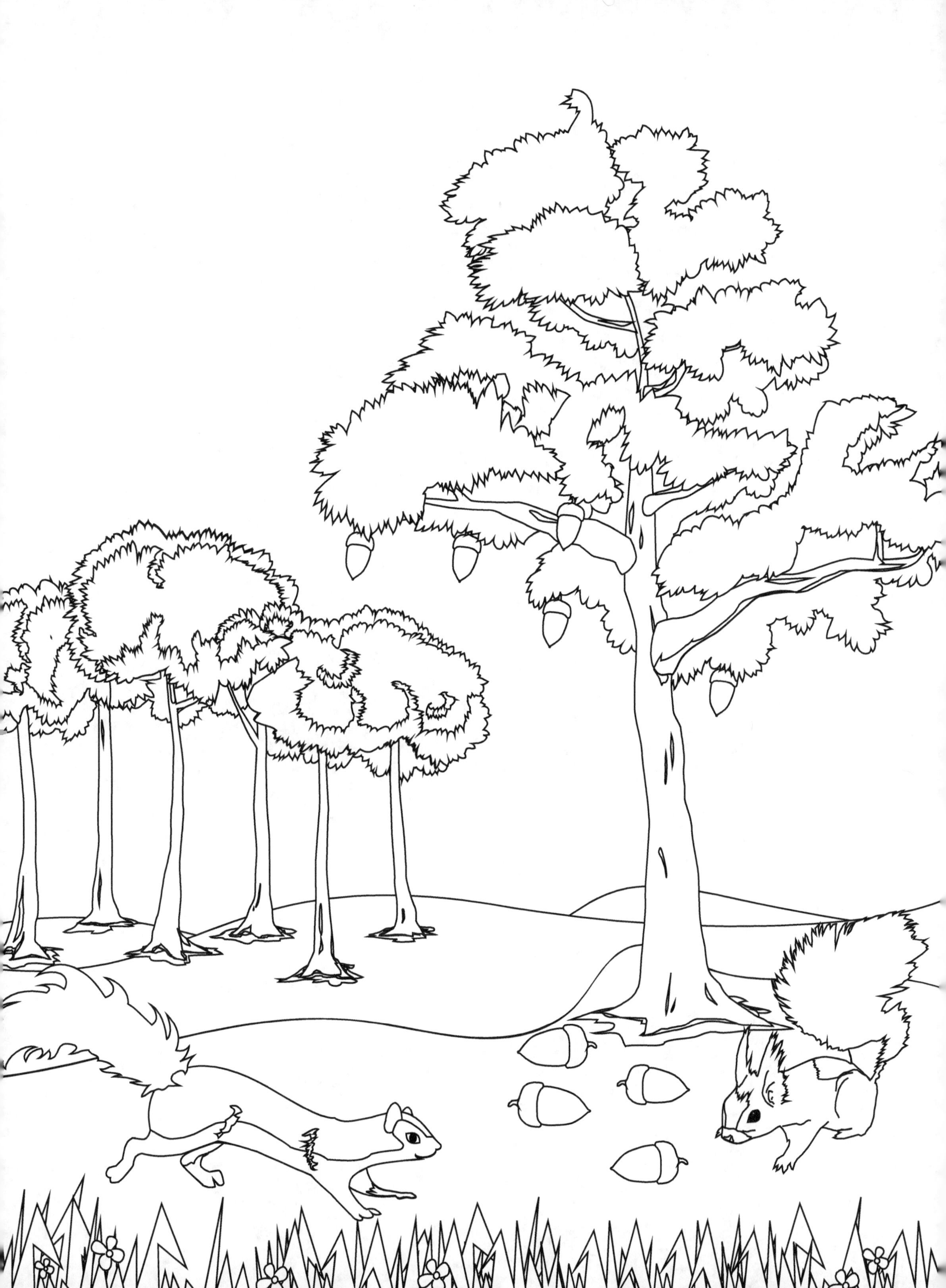

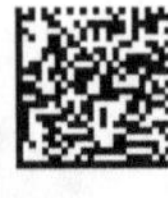
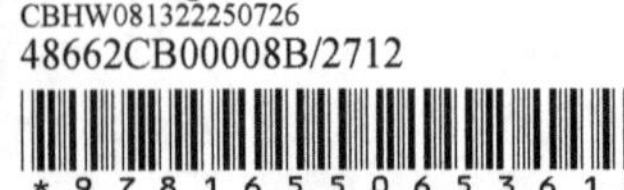